RELAX!

This Book is Only a Phase You're Going Through

by Charles Ortleb and Richard Fiala

St. Martin's Press, Inc. New York, N.Y.

For information, write:
St. Martin's Press
175 Fifth Avenue
New York, N.Y. 10010
Manufactured in the United States of America
Library of Congress Catalog Card Number:

Library of Congress Cataloging in Publication Data

Ortleb, Charles.
  Relax! : This book is only a phase you're going
through.

  1. Homosexuality—Caricatures and cartoons.
2. American wit and humor, Pictorial. I. Fiala,
Richard, joint author. II. Christopher Street.
III. Title.
NC1428.C48077   741.5′973   78-3978
ISBN 0-312-67046-X
ISBN 0-312-67047-8 prepack

NOTE: All cartoons drawn by Richard Fiala, including those signed "Lublin" and "(Bertram) Dusk."

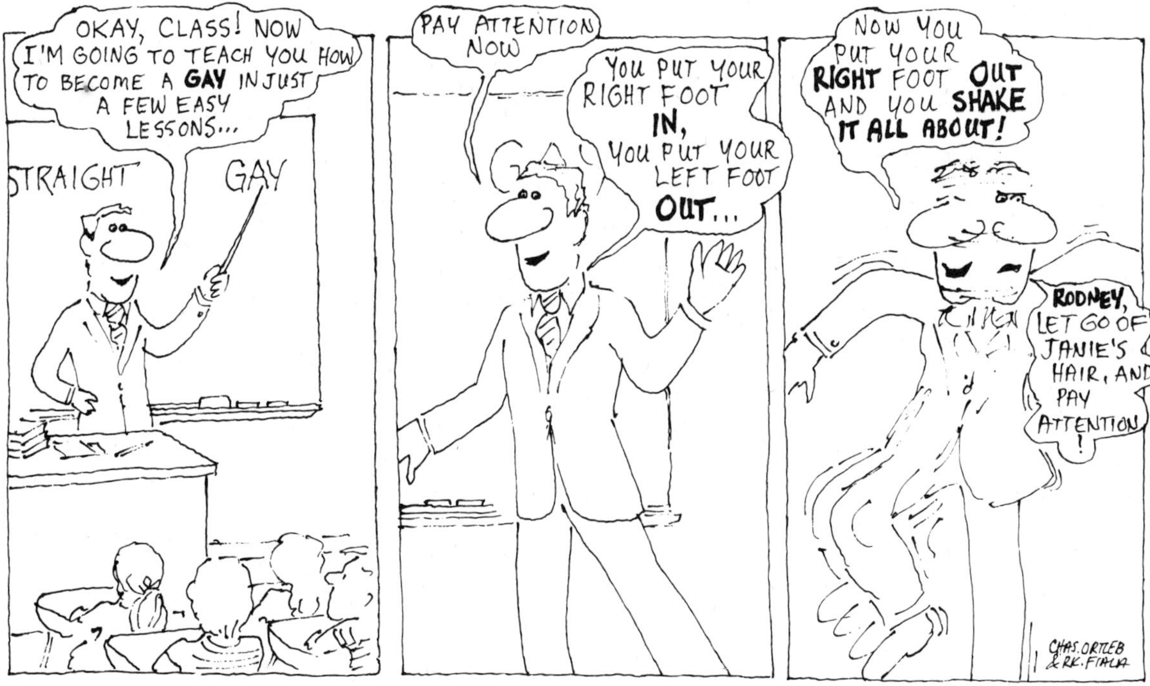

OKAY, CLASS! NOW I'M GOING TO TEACH YOU HOW TO BECOME A **GAY** IN JUST A FEW EASY LESSONS...
STRAIGHT
GAY
PAY ATTENTION NOW
YOU PUT YOUR RIGHT FOOT **IN,** YOU PUT YOUR LEFT FOOT **OUT**...
NOW YOU PUT YOUR **RIGHT** FOOT **OUT** AND YOU **SHAKE IT ALL ABOUT!**
RODNEY, LET GO OF JANIE'S HAIR, AND PAY ATTENTION!
CHAS. ORTLEB & RK. FIALA

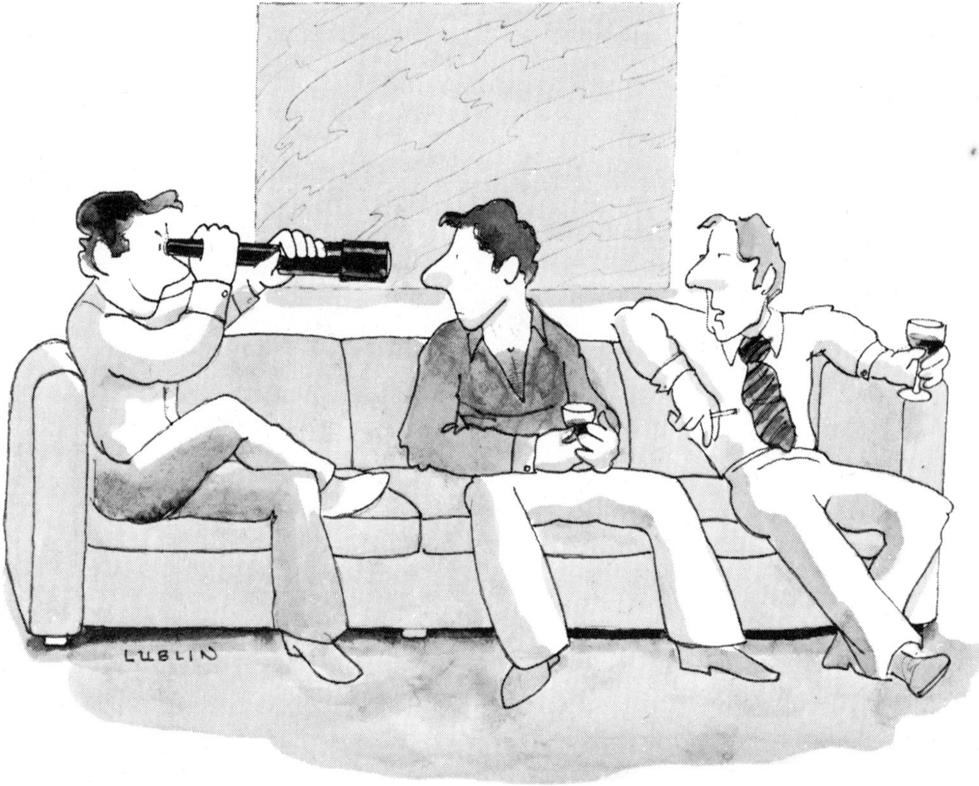
LUBLIN

"Men fascinate him."

"If you leave me now, all you'll get is a life full of facsimiles."

"Perrier and yogurt! Perrier and yogurt! Is that all you gay people eat—Perrier and yogurt?"

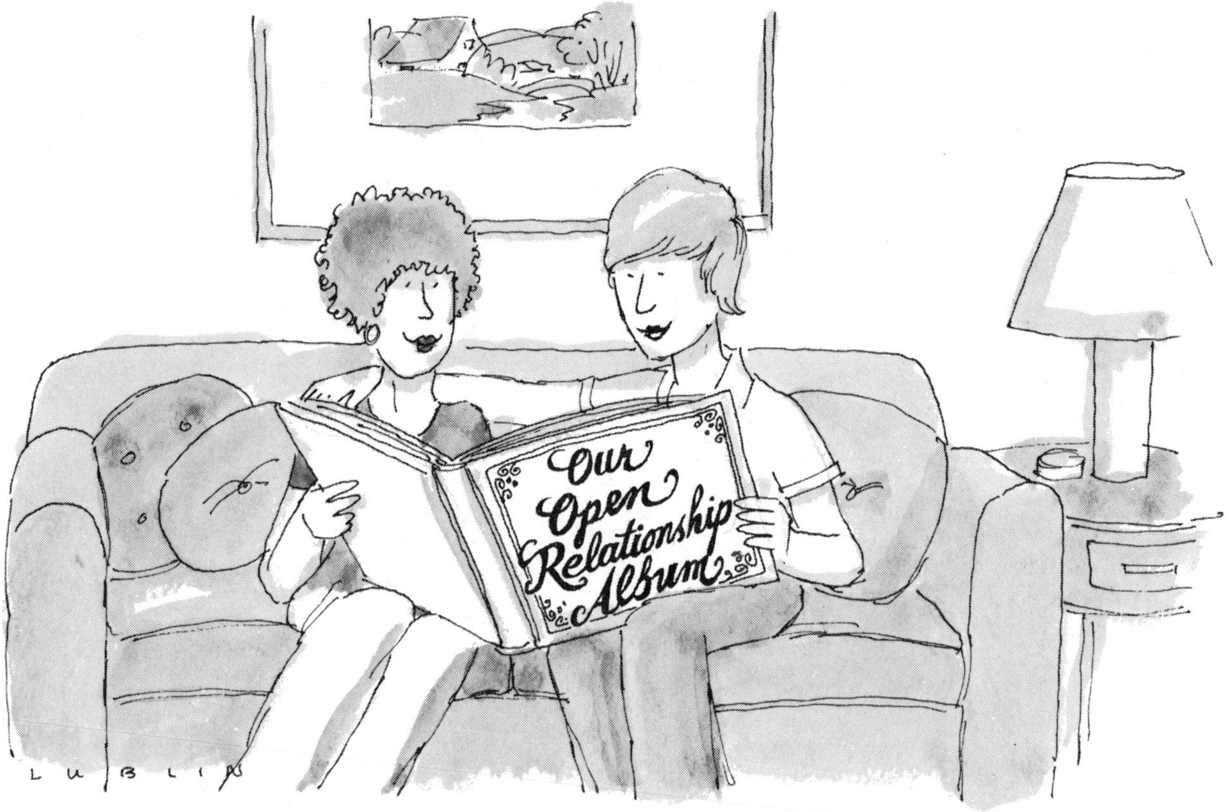
Our Open Relationship Album
LUBLIN

"Michael, what you're seeing is one of the weak points of our relationship."

LOOKING FOR A STRAIGHT TABLE IN A GAY RESTAURANT.

A SCIENTIST DISCOVERS HOMOSEXUALITY AMONG HIS LABORATORY MICE.

". . . then I dumped Utah Axe after it split and bought
Agro-Am Machines on the advice of my broker at 3½. It's
now at 7¼, so I might sell and buy up what would amount
to controlling interest in a promising little outfit called
Oceanic Spoll & Bobbin, which is diversifying into fodder
products and book publishing . . ."

REPORT CARD

LORD ALFRED DOUGLAS ELEMENTARY SCHOOL

Name: Lawrence Wentworth, Jr.

E = EXCELLENT **S** = SATISFACTORY **U** = UNSAT.

	S
Taste	E
Haughtiness & Petulance	E
Making Entrances & Exits	E
Cleverness in Getting out of Phys. Ed.	S
Furtive Glances	E
Venomous Remarks	E
Excessive Tidiness	E

Remarks: Little Lawrence is a credit to Lord Alfred Douglas Elementary School. You should be very proud of him.

P.D. McAnn
L's Teacher

RICK FIALA

"Really, Miss Wells, there's got to be a better way of telling us how big the gay market is."

"Must you always be manic when I'm depressive?"

AN APARTMENT
HOUSE ON THE EAST SIDE
FOR GAY MEN
WHO LIKE TO VISIT
EACHOTHER OFTEN

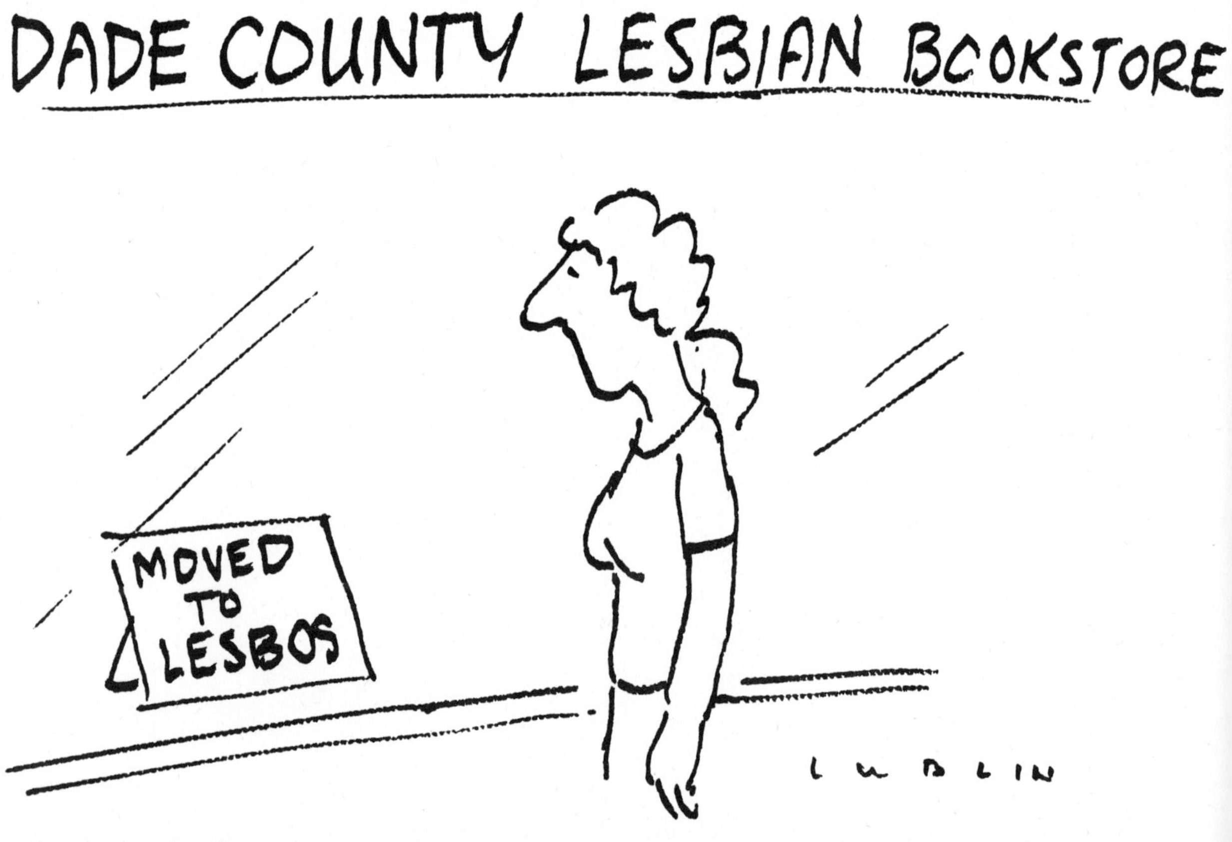
DADE COUNTY LESBIAN BOOKSTORE
MOVED TO LESBOS
LUBLIN

"But we'd still like two seats together, thank you."

MEN
WOMEN
BEST OF BOTH WORLDS
RICK FIPLA

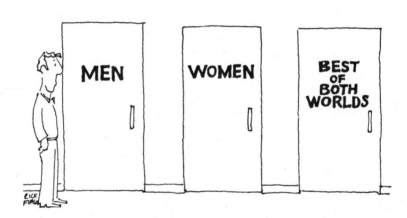

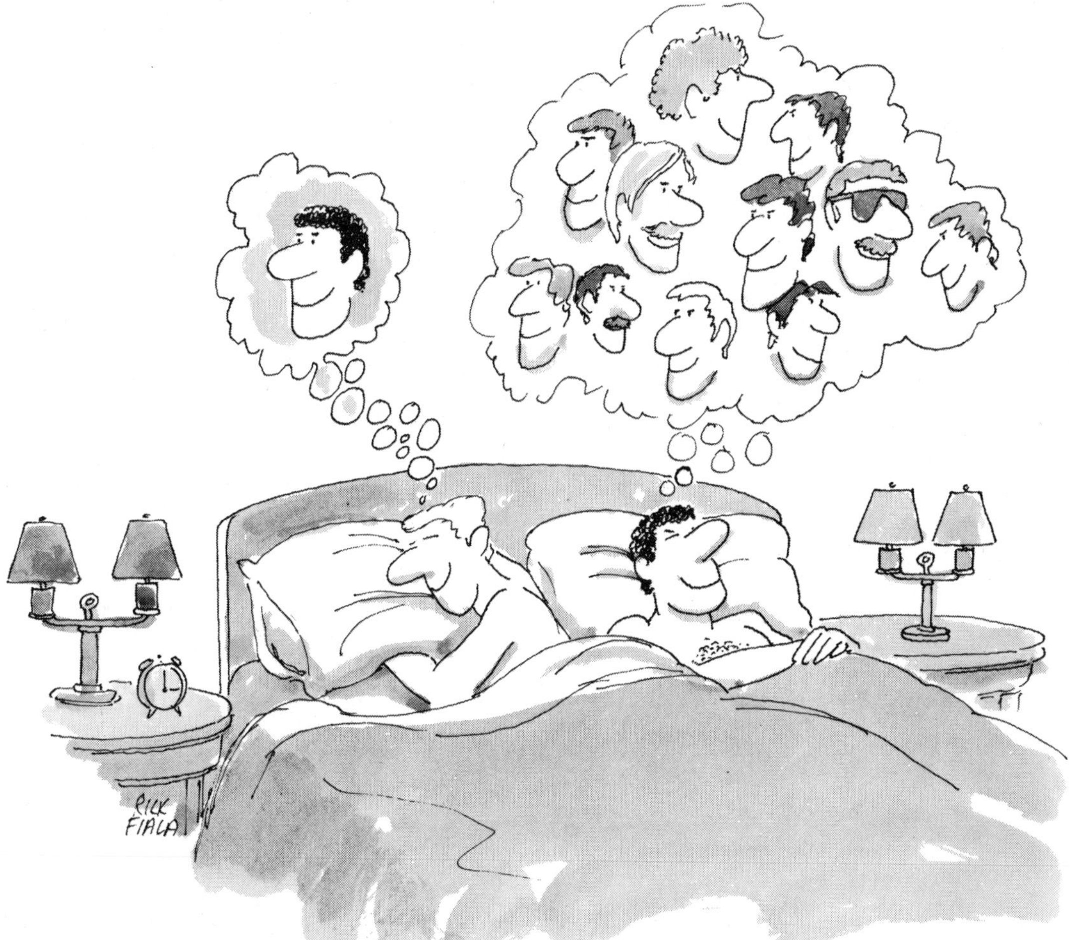
RICK
FIALA

"Mother, you remember Sally. We came out together in '68."

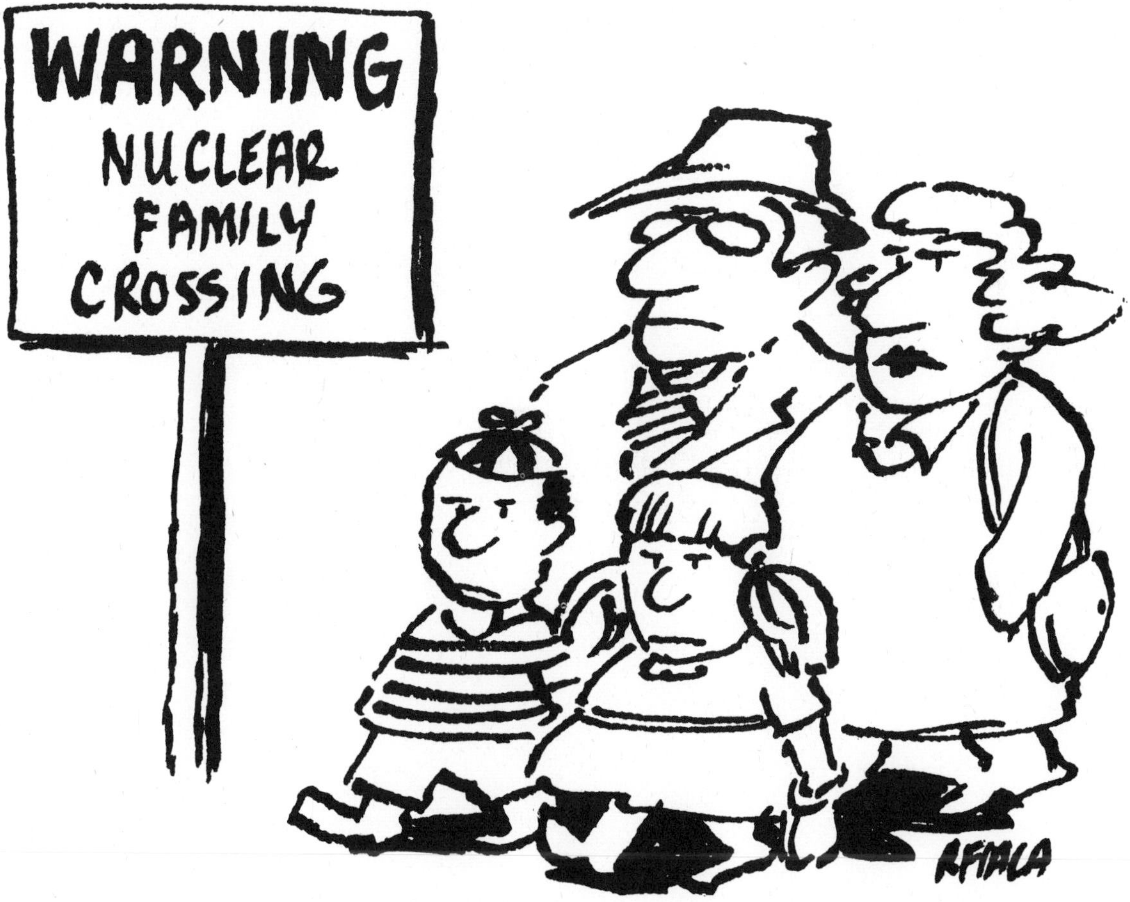
WARNING
NUCLEAR
FAMILY
CROSSING
RFIALA

"Now, don't get us wrong, Mr. Garrett. We at First National are just as excited about that dream house out at The Pines as you are . . ."

FRED AND MAC, HAVING DECIDED TO BREAK UP
AFTER LIVING TOGETHER FOR THREE YEARS,
PREPARE TO DIVIDE THE MOPED.

IN EACH OF THE ABOVE GROUPS OF PROFESSIONALS, CAN YOU IDENTIFY THE ONE GAY PERSON TRYING TO PASS AS STRAIGHT?

"I throw one of these every summer to bring gay men and lesbians back together again."

"Distant father, close-binding mother."

"I don't require much to be happy: a jug of wine, a stereo, a skylight—and thou."

VETERAN PARTY-THROWER ALICE BROWN DISPENSES WITH THE USUAL NAMETAGS AND DECIDES THAT EVERYONE SHOULD GET TO THE POINT.

"Don't worry, I'm wearing a leisure suit under this."

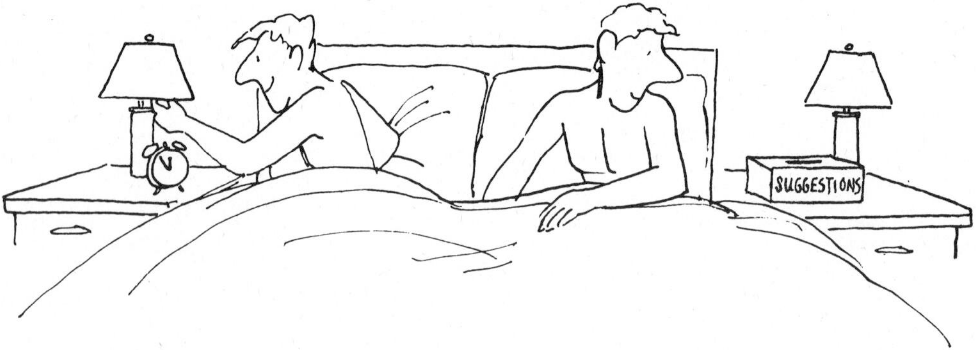
SUGGESTIONS

(1.)

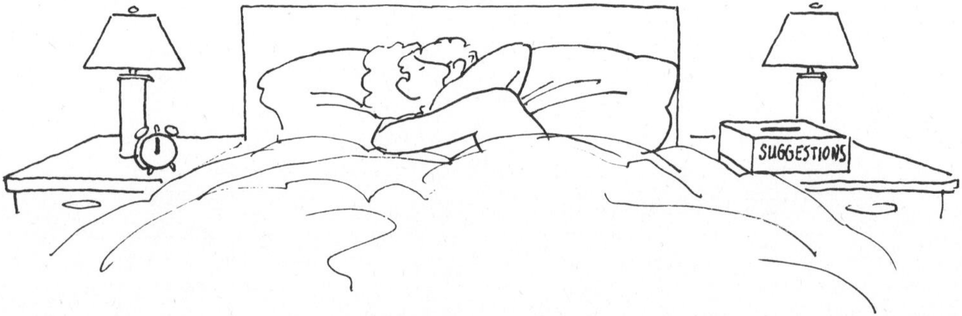
SUGGESTIONS

(2.)

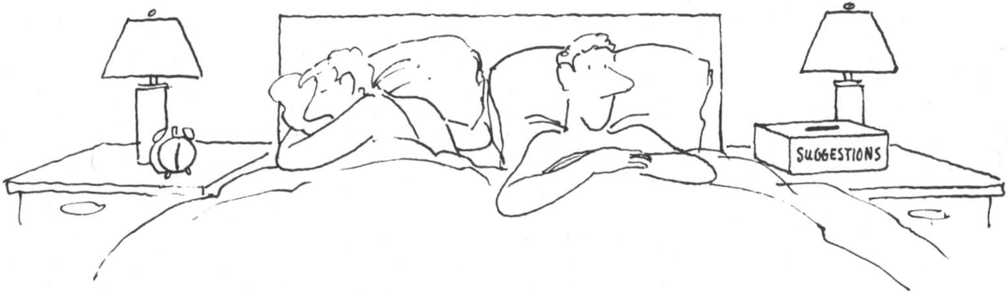
SUGGESTIONS

(3.)

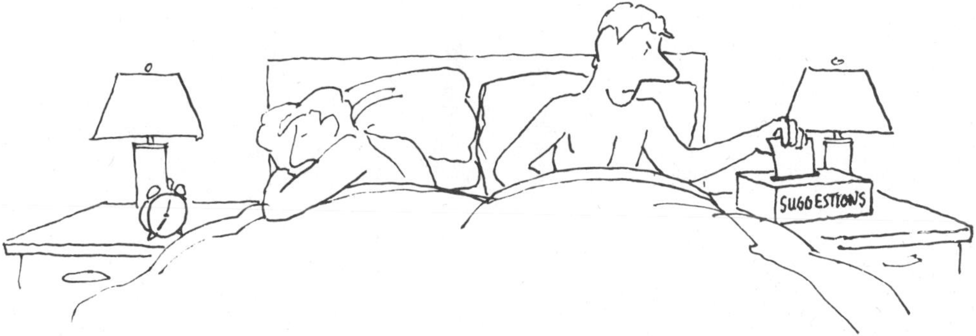
SUGGESTIONS

(4.)

"It's your mother. I think she wants to cut off all diplomatic ties again."

TODD MACNAMARA SHOWS HIS LOVER TIM
THE LONG-AWAITED BACKLASH THAT LIBERALS
HAVE PREDICTED FOR YEARS.

PSYCHOLOGISTS HAVE SHOWN THAT
THE WAY WE SLEEP INDICATES THE WAY
WE LIVE

"Wanna go home and play Cowboys and Waterbeds?"

"This idea of Anita Bryant's is fabulous!"

"I don't want casual sex—I want a nexus."

"*So when did you first become conscious of being oppressed because of your homosexuality?*"

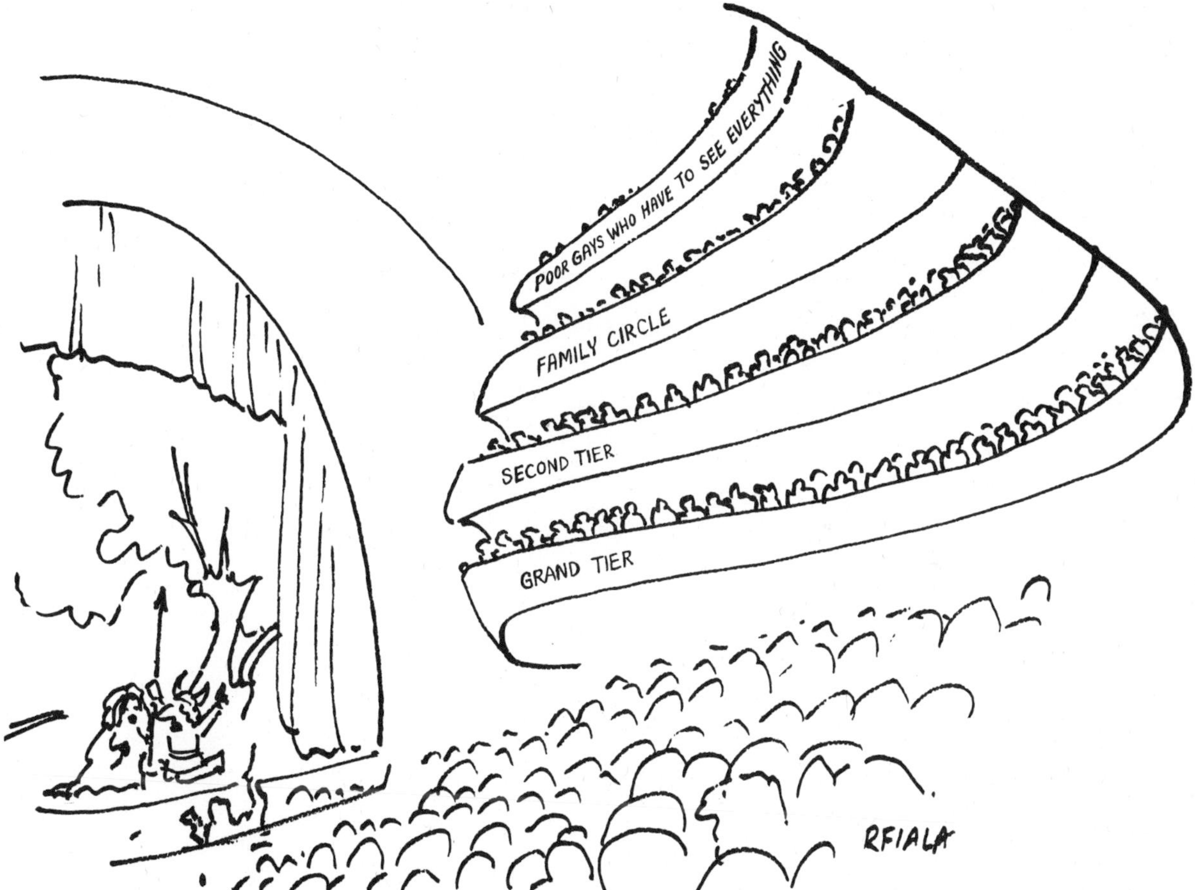
POOR GAYS WHO HAVE TO SEE EVERYTHING
FAMILY CIRCLE
SECOND TIER
GRAND TIER
RFIALA

"Sorry, Jerry, mood rings never lie."

"To the same sex—whenever, wherever!"

"Oh, terrific. We're going to have to hear yet another *coming-out story."*

"I told you shopping on Fire Island would be an unusual experience."

"*I guess I overdid the bronzer.*"

TWO NEW BOOKS FIND THEIR MARKETS.

"I didn't say it takes all kinds, Roger. I said you *do."*

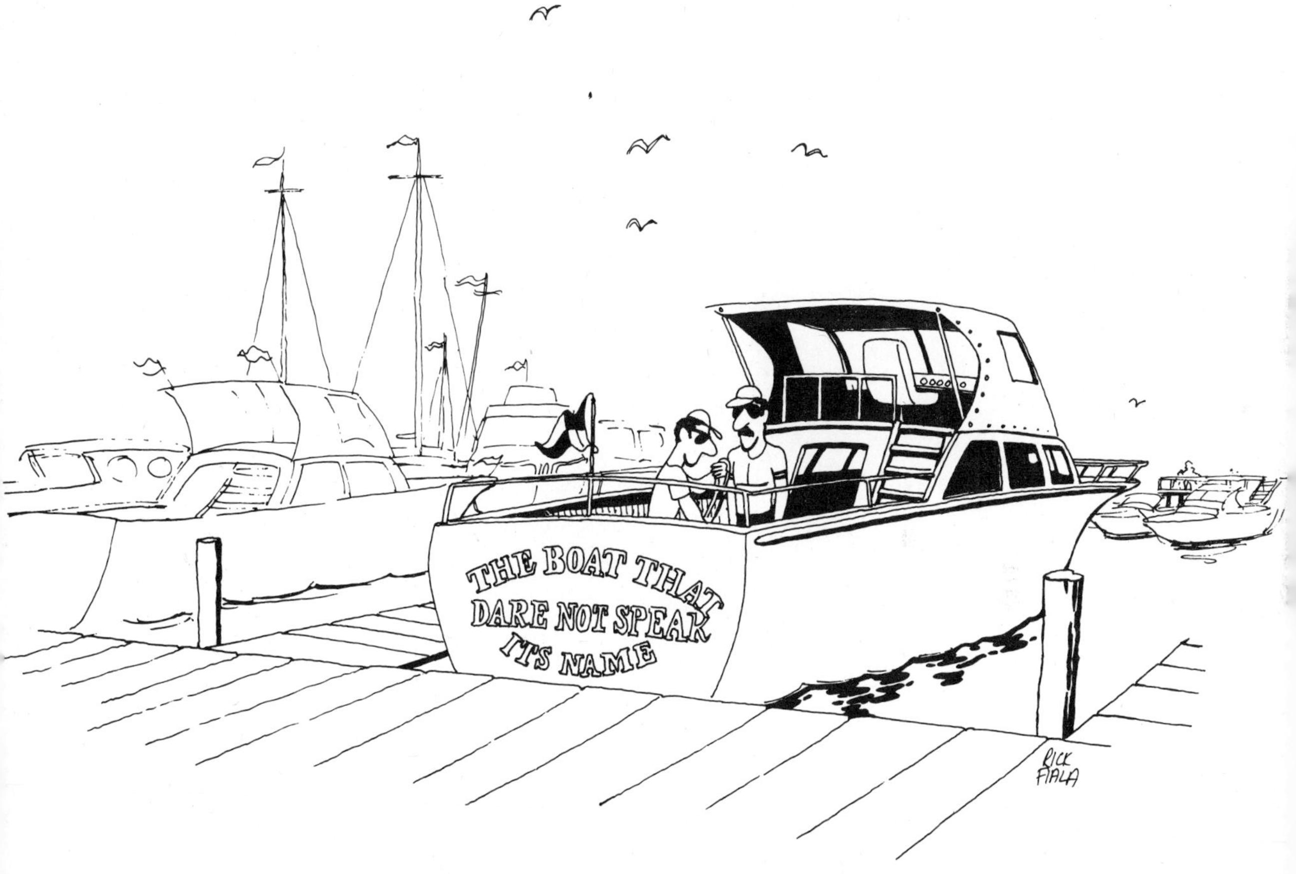

THE BOAT THAT
DARE NOT SPEAK
IT'S NAME
RICK FIALA

"Well, you don't look so good to me, either."

"If you can't get it in New York, you can't get it."

" 'Lover' may be too strong a term. Let's just say we live under the same rock."

*"Look, Betty, it's just that I'm only at-
tracted to people who* don't *jog."*

...THE FIRST APPROPRIATELY NAMED GAY BAR.

"Honey, this is Gary. Gary is gay, and we've just been comparing oppressions."

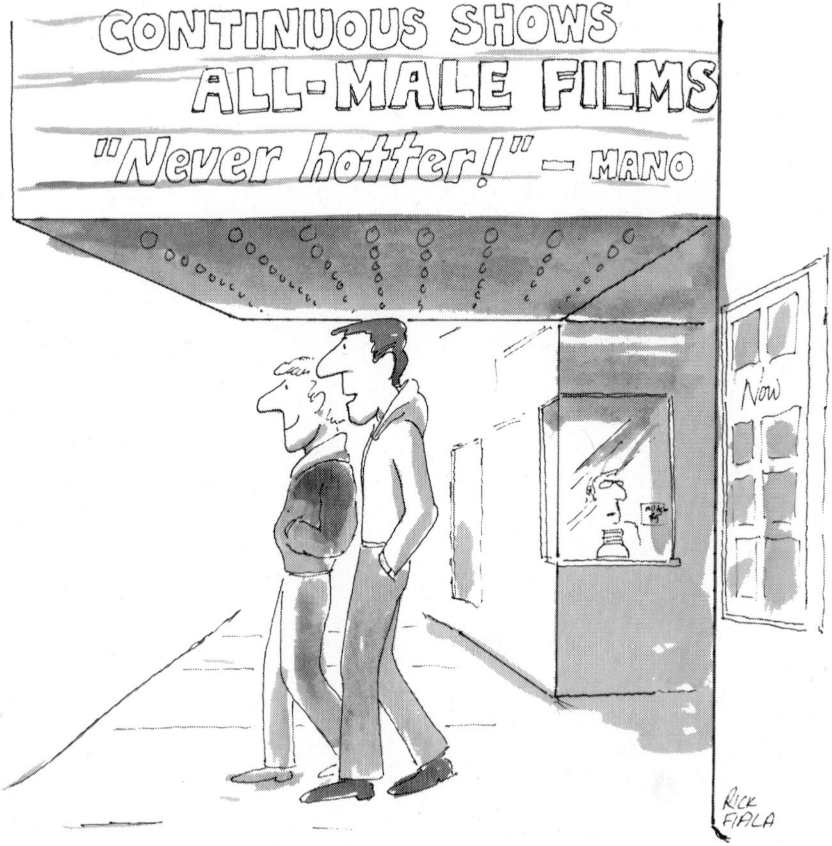
CONTINUOUS SHOWS
ALL-MALE FILMS
"Never hotter!" — MANO
Now
RICK FIALA

"Loved *him*. Hated *him*."

COACH WALDERMAN
PASSES OUT XEROXES OF AN
ARTICLE ASSERTING THAT ONLY
ONE IN TEN OF HIS TEAM
COULD POSSIBLY BE GAY.

"I never had to dig for crabs."

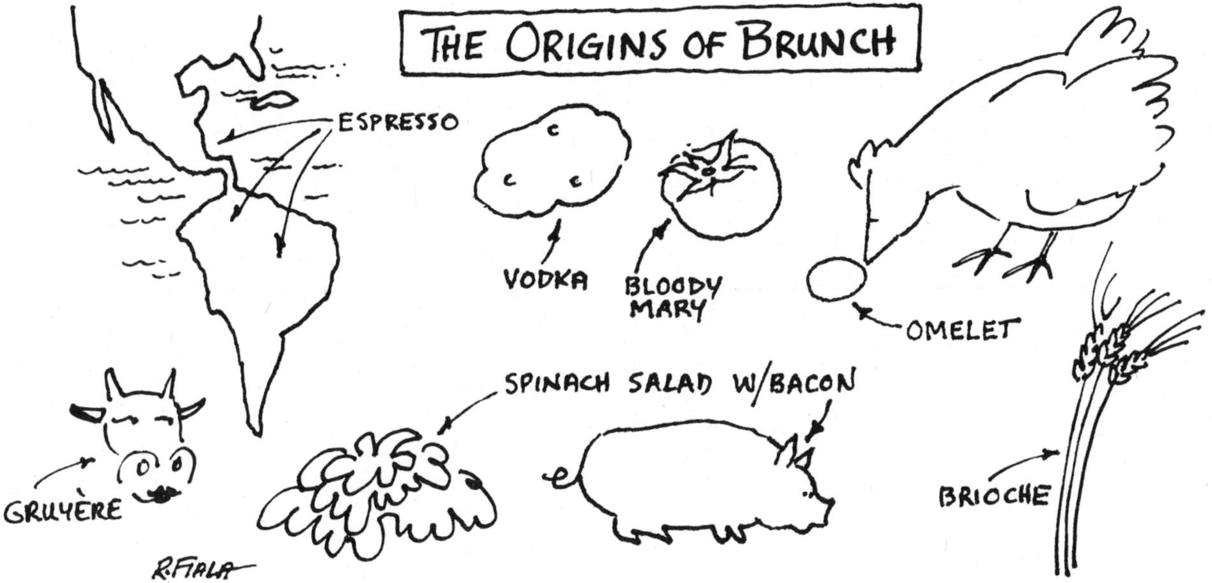

THE ORIGINS OF BRUNCH
ESPRESSO
VODKA
BLOODY MARY
OMELET
SPINACH SALAD W/BACON
GRUYÈRE
BRIOCHE
R.FIALA

AN AGENT FROM THE BLAKE MANAGEMENT CO. INFORMS
RESIDENTS THAT THE GOLDEN YEARS HOTEL IS BEING
RENAMED "STUD CORRAL", AND THEY HAVE TWO WEEKS
TO MOVE OUT.

"Thank you, Marion, for raising my consciousness. Now leave."

A GAY PERSON INTERVIEWING A GROUP OF
DAVID SUSSKINDS.

"Oh, I thought I'd just throw on a workshirt, and go out and make it with the proletariat."

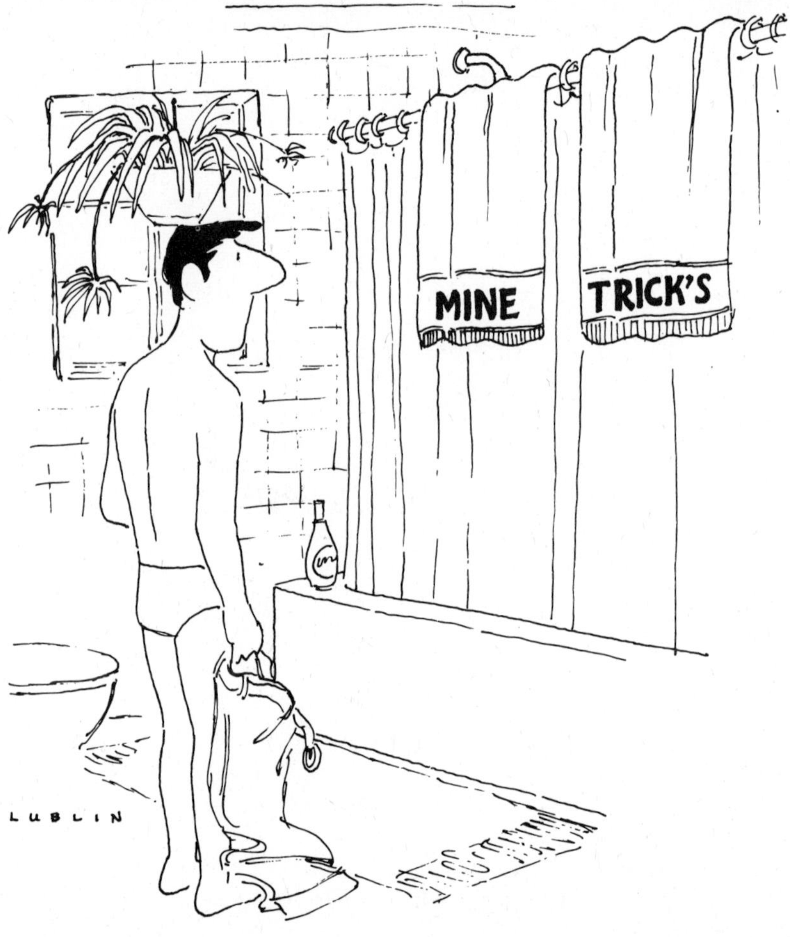
MINE
TRICK'S
LUBLIN

"Mother, do Jeff and I have to know everything you do *in bed?"*

QUIET...
GAY COUPLES
LISTENING TO
MOZART

"I know it must strike you a little odd that two single men in Gucci shoes want to rent your one-bedroom apartment, Mrs. Dellwood, but times are hard."

IT IS FOUR IN THE MORNING. AS GAY MEN ARE RETURNING HOME FROM THE BARS ON THE LEXINGTON AVENUE LINE, A WISTFULL THIRTY-FIVE YEAR-OLD MAN STANDS UP AND SINGS "WHAT *I* DID FOR LOVE."

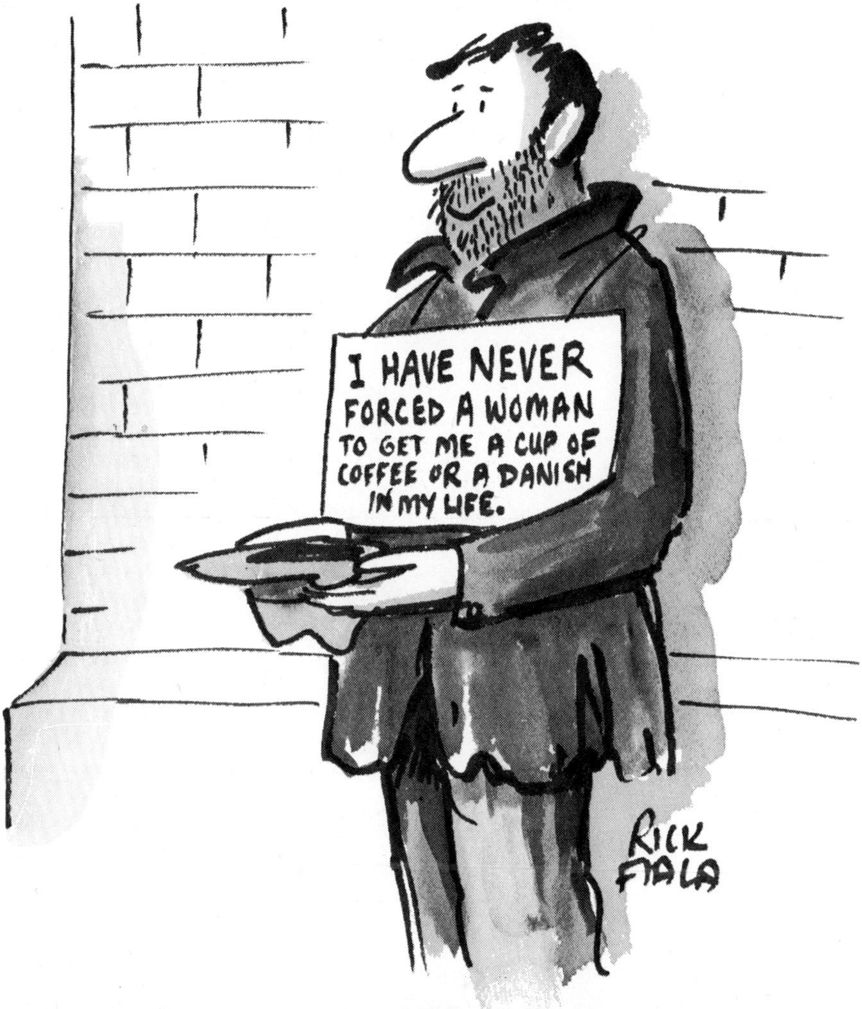
I HAVE NEVER FORCED A WOMAN TO GET ME A CUP OF COFFEE OR A DANISH IN MY LIFE.
RICK FIALA

"Okay! Okay! You want plastic slipcovers, you got plastic slipcovers!"

"Actor/Model/Waiter!   Actor/Model/Waiter!"

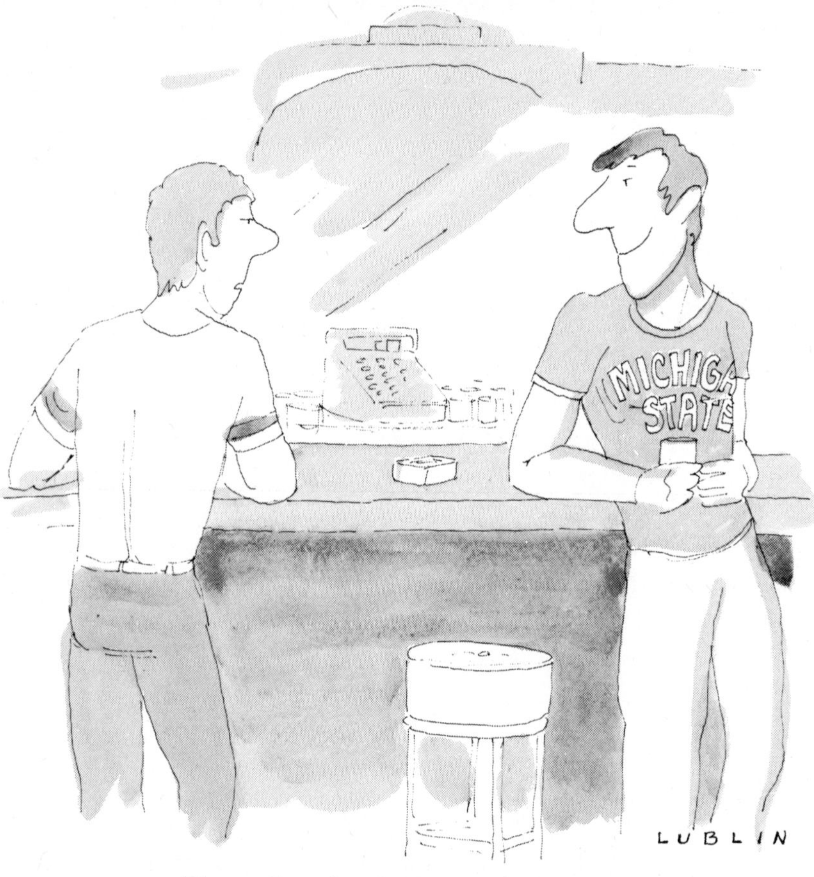
MICHIGA
STATE
LUBLIN

"Sorry, I've already slept with the Big Ten."

"I would've taken part in the looting during the Blackout,
but I couldn't get up to Bloomingdale's."

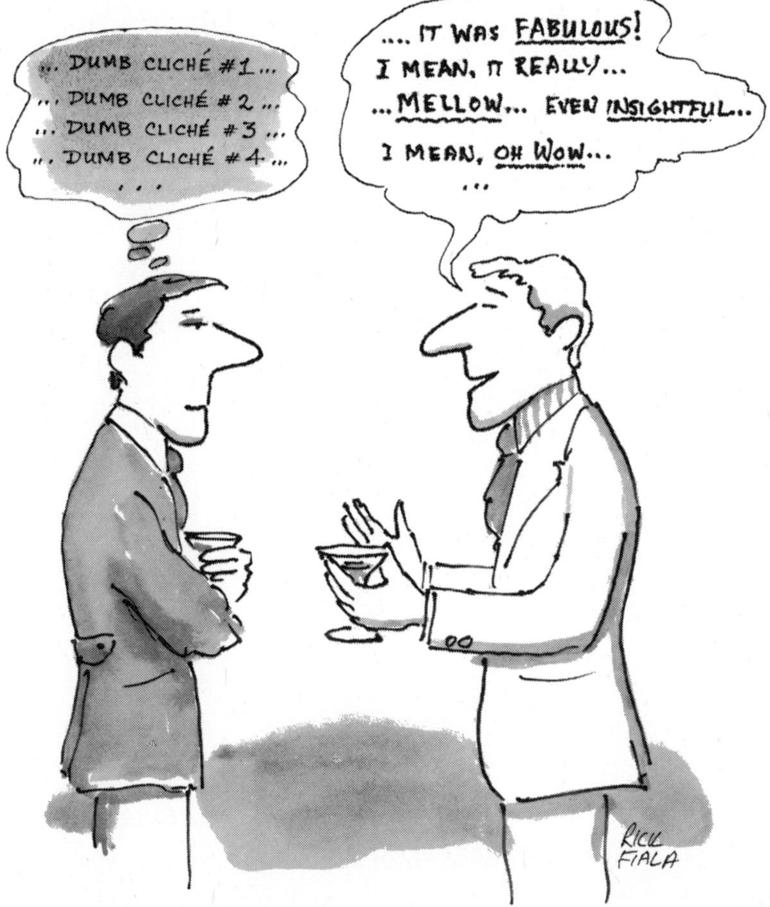
... DUMB CLICHÉ #1...
... DUMB CLICHÉ #2...
... DUMB CLICHÉ #3...
... DUMB CLICHÉ #4...
...
.... IT WAS FABULOUS!
I MEAN, IT REALLY...
...MELLOW... EVEN INSIGHTFUL...
I MEAN, OH WOW...
...
RICK FIALA

"This is not the style in which I am accustomed to being abandoned."

"It's my parents. Quick, help me think of something heterosexual to say."

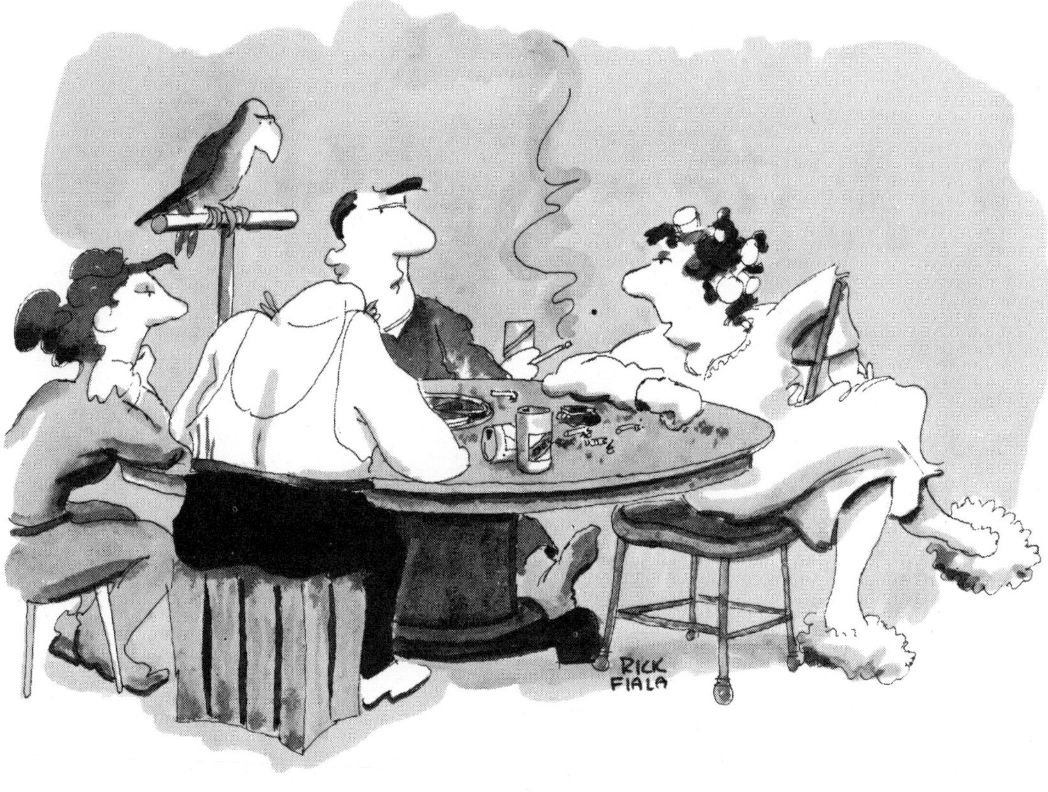
RICK
FIALA

"If it wasn't for the beer and the pizza, we might be mistaken for the Bloomsbury Group."

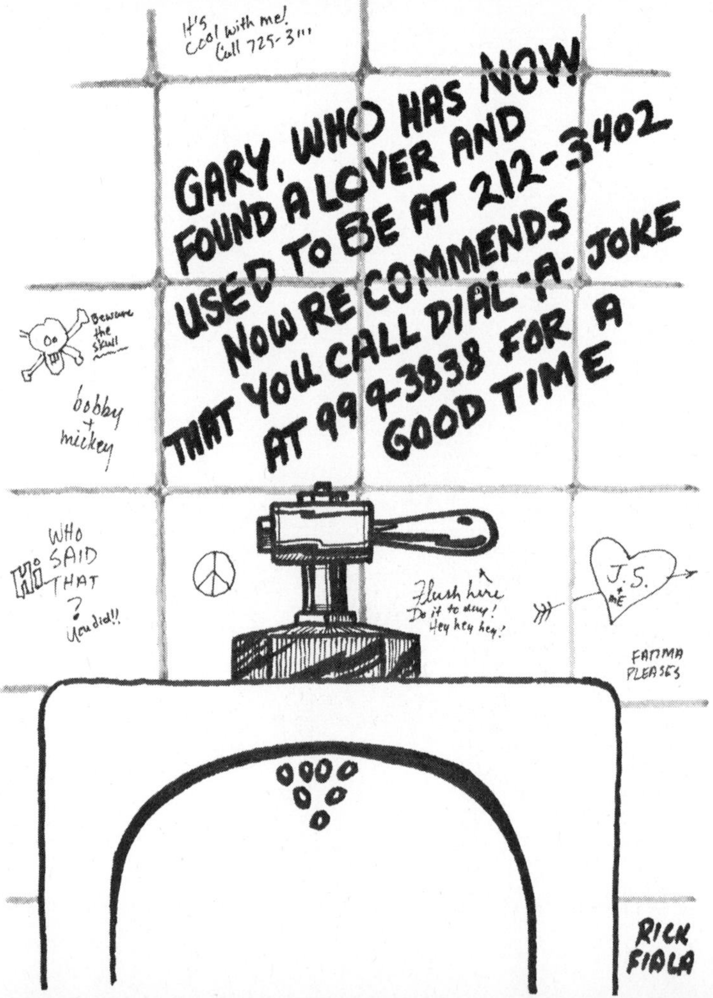
It's cool with me! Call 725-3'''
GARY, WHO HAS NOW FOUND A LOVER AND USED TO BE AT 212-3402 NOW RECOMMENDS THAT YOU CALL DIAL-A-JOKE AT 999-3838 FOR A GOOD TIME
Beware the skull
bobby + mickey
Hi
WHO SAID THAT ?
You did!!
Flush here
Do it to day!
Hey hey hey!
J.S. + ME
FATIMA PLEASES
RICK FIALA

"I guess you're all wondering why I called you here."

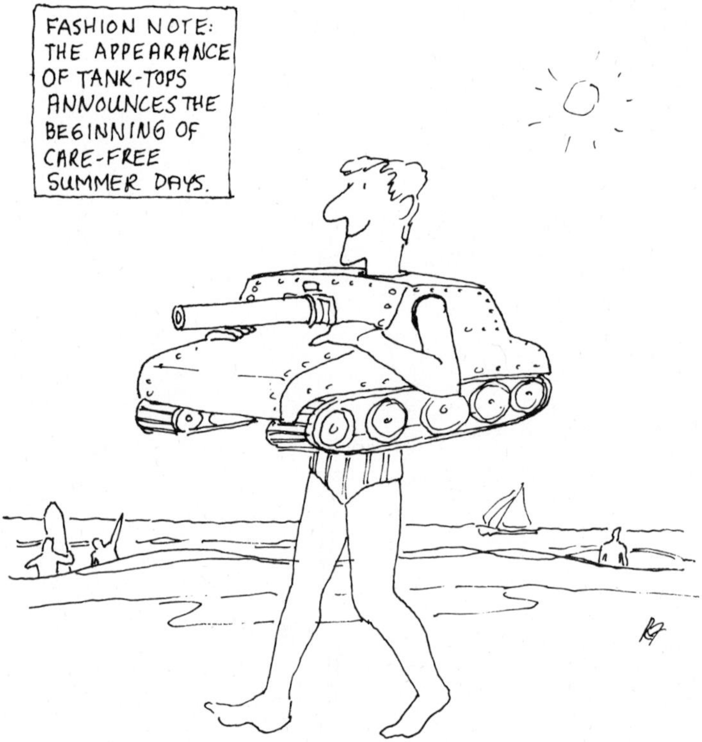
FASHION NOTE: THE APPEARANCE OF TANK-TOPS ANNOUNCES THE BEGINNING OF CARE-FREE SUMMER DAYS.

"Yes, little Jeffrey turned out to be quite normal, but we're coping well with the disappointment."

"Well, as The New York Times would put it, we're sharing the same apartment."

"I dreamt I ordered a Jac-Pack, but instead they sent me a Vegematic."

"*Don't be afraid. Just think of it as going to that Big Disco in the sky.*"

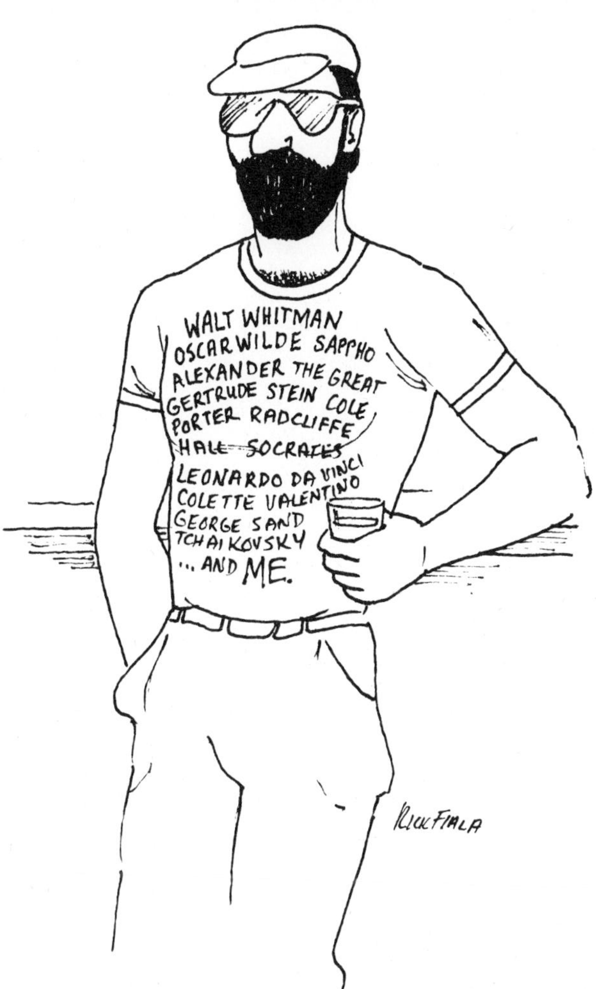
WALT WHITMAN
OSCAR WILDE SAPPHO
ALEXANDER THE GREAT
GERTRUDE STEIN COLE
PORTER RADCLIFFE
HALL SOCRATES
LEONARDO DA VINCI
COLETTE VALENTINO
GEORGE SAND
TCHAIKOVSKY
... AND ME.
RICK FIALA

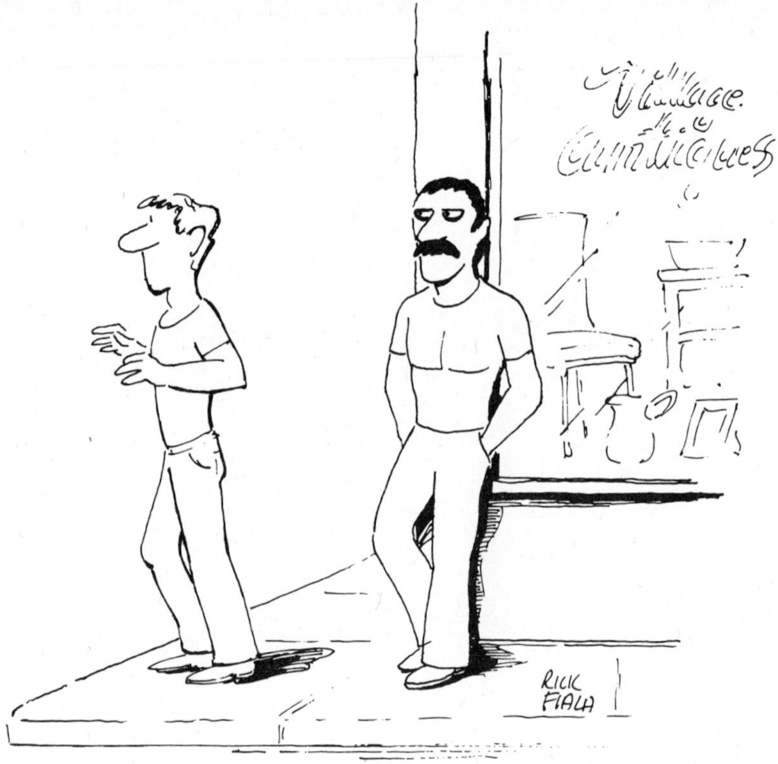
RICK
FIALA

THOUGH FACED IN THE OPPOSITE DIRECTION, AN INNOCENT PASSERBY IS STOPPED DEAD IN HIS TRACKS BY AL "THE-CRUISE-OF-DEATH" JONES.

"How about coming over for a few drinks and a little media?"

"*Janie, I've decided to go straight.*"

"Every time you have an orgasm, I feel like notifying your next of kin."

"So then I threw her on the bed, and I said, 'Look, Mabel, I am now issuing my own Hite Report!'"

"I told you to grab a lover and get back to your apartment before winter started!"

"Elliot, I'd like you to meet Mrs. Fremont Nelson. Mrs. Nelson is a gay people buff."

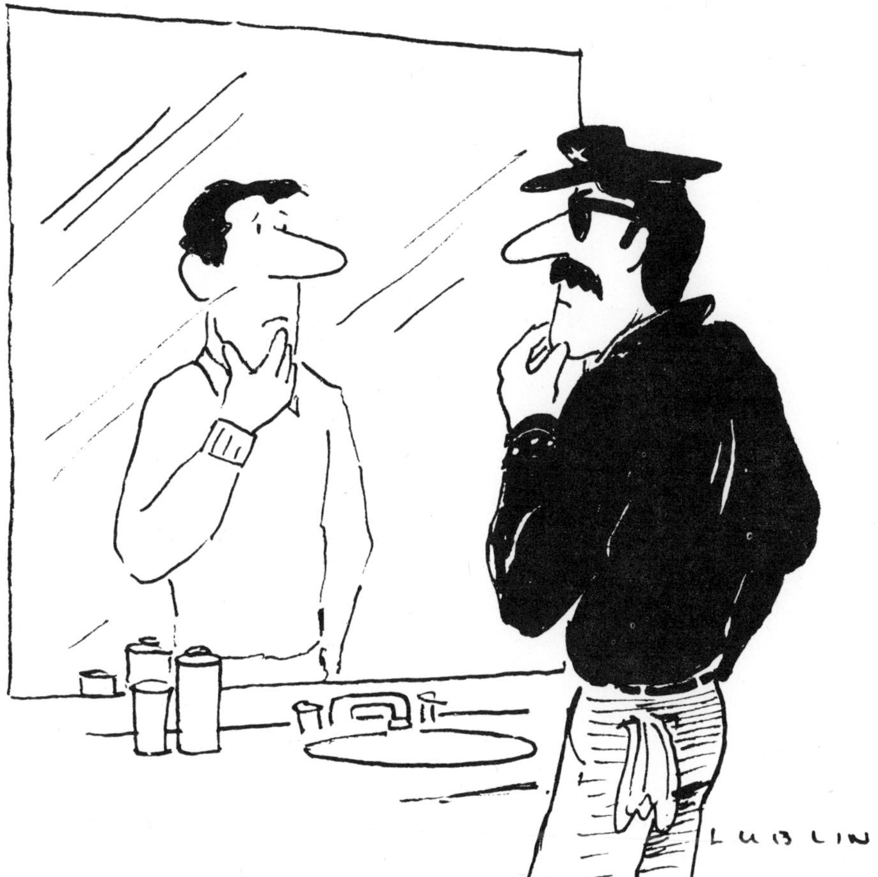
LUBLIN

"What's it going to be tonight—feeling or technique?"

"As you know, I've been living in a ménage à trois. I'd like you to meet my other third."

"If you wouldn't do it in a hundred-dollar-a-night room last night, I certainly have no intention of doing it on an overrated beach today!"

"Okay, so which bar do you want to be a new face in tonight?"

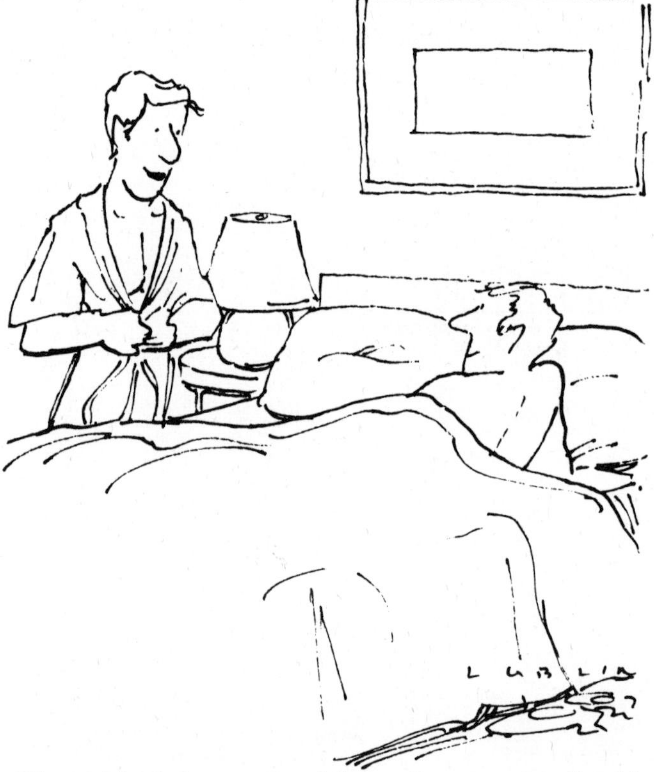
LUBLIN

"Last night I dreamt that Johnny Carson stopped asking gay entertainers when they were getting married."

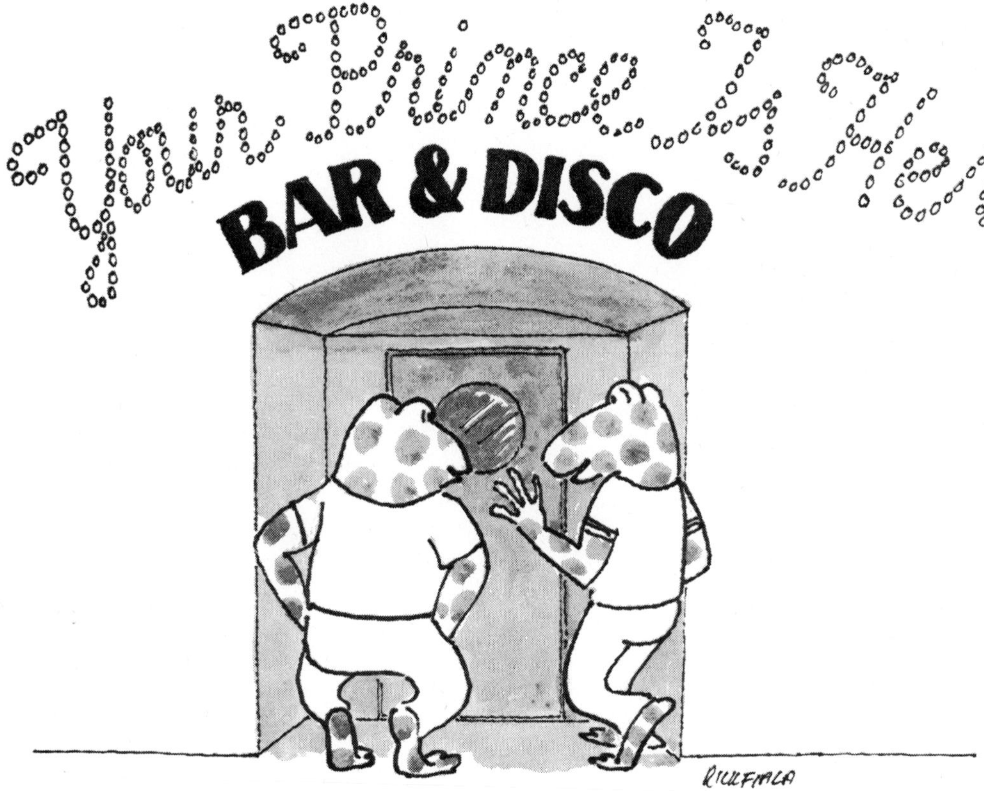
Your Prince Is Here.
BAR & DISCO
RICK FIALA

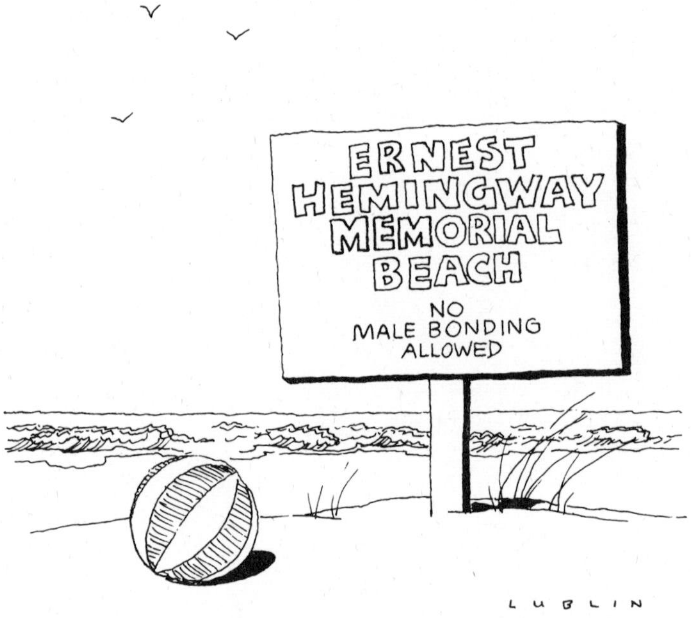
ERNEST
HEMINGWAY
MEMORIAL
BEACH
NO
MALE BONDING
ALLOWED
LUBLIN

"You keep the kids—I want the shoe."

"Sorry, but you used up all your Virginia Woolf
quotes in the last argument we had."

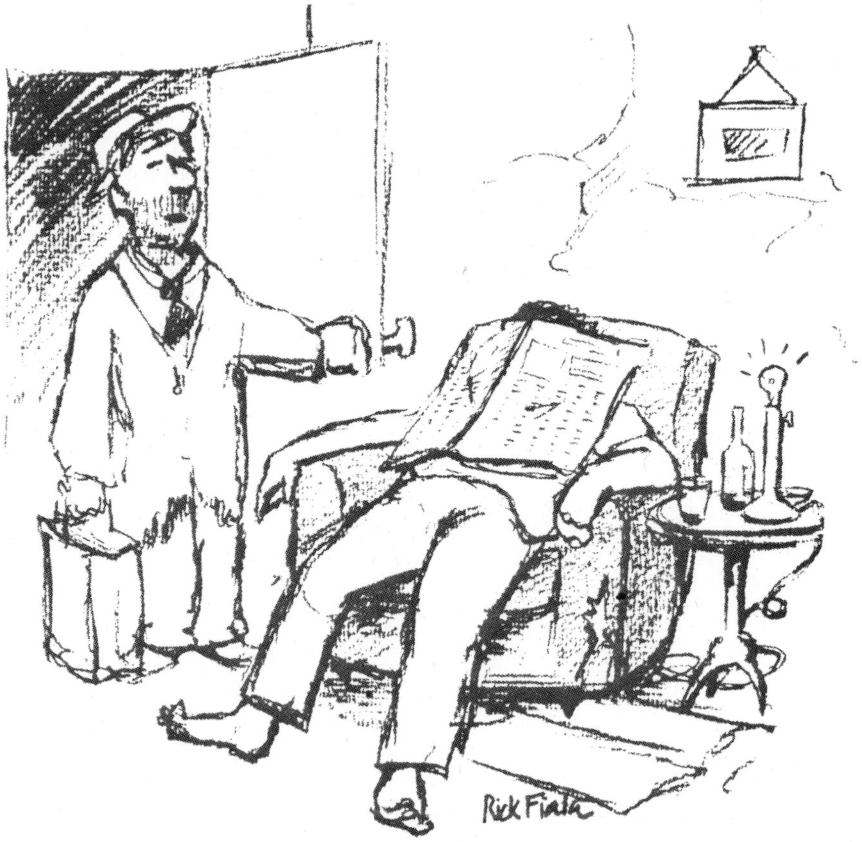
Rick Fiala

"Je reviens."

"I'm glad we met at the bar last night. In case we never meet again, May the Force Be With You."

UNABLE TO BRING HIMSELF TO LEAVE THE PINES AT THE END OF THE SEASON, CALVIN ZENDER WINTERIZES HIMSELF.

"So this is your immortal quiche."

"When Mother accepts something, she goes all the way."

"*I've always been partial to films that make me think.*"

"Unfortunately, my lover has finally found his niche."

A MAJOR AMERICAN
CANDY MANUFACTURER SWITCHES
ITS MARKETING STRATEGY.

"Face it, Bill, even after you lose twenty pounds, there will still be ten layers of ambiguity."

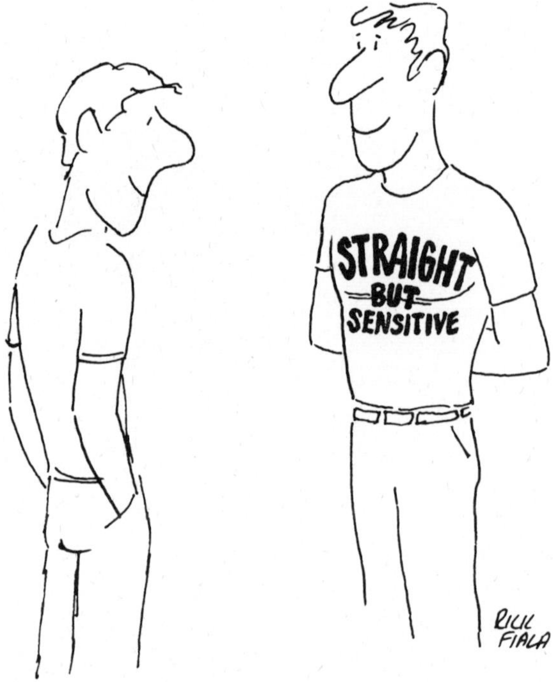
STRAIGHT
BUT
SENSITIVE
RICK
FIALA